Sentinel

Other Books by Robert Hunter

Night Cadre
Idiot's Delight
Infinity Minus Eleven
A Box of Rain: Lyrics 1965–1993

Translations

Duino Elegies,
by Rainer Maria Rilke

The Sonnets to Orpheus,
by Rainer Maria Rilke

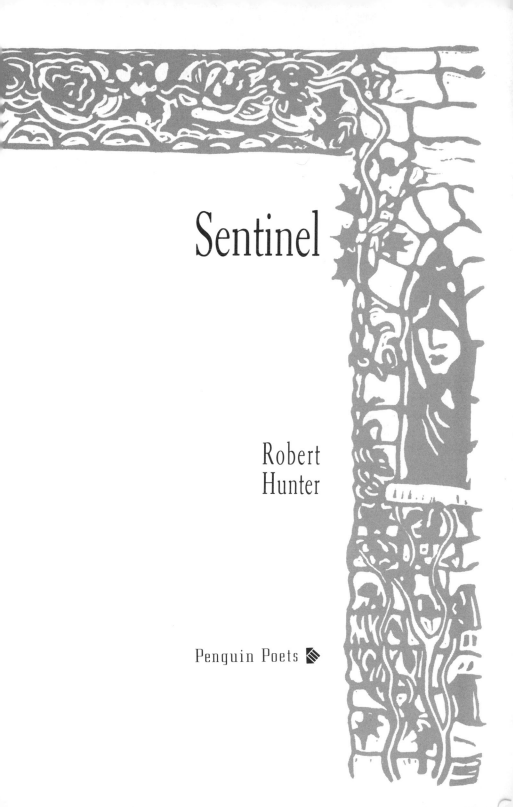

Sentinel

Robert
Hunter

Penguin Poets

PENGUIN BOOKS

Published by the Penguin Group
Penguin Books USA Inc., 375 Hudson Street,
New York, New York 10014, U.S.A.
Penguin Books Ltd, 27 Wrights Lane, London W8 5TZ, England
Penguin Books Australia Ltd, Ringwood, Victoria, Australia
Penguin Books Canada Ltd, 10 Alcorn Avenue,
Toronto, Ontario, Canada M4V 3B2
Penguin Books (N.Z.) Ltd, 182–190 Wairau Road,
Auckland 10, New Zealand

Penguin Books Ltd, Registered Offices:
Harmondsworth, Middlesex, England

First published in Penguin Books 1993

1 2 3 4 5 6 7 8 9 10

LIBRARY OF CONGRESS CATALOGING IN PUBLICATION DATA
Hunter, Robert.
Sentinel/by Robert Hunter.
p. cm.
ISBN 0 14 058.698 9
I. Title.
PS3558.U489S46   1993
811'.54—dc20   93–12968

Printed in the United States of America
Set in Electra
Designed by Cheryl L. Cipriani

CONTENTS

Sentinel

A Red Dog's Decoration Day

A red dog trots down Divisidero
longing for a new creation.
He crosses Fillmore seeking
a new logic and
new ends to meaning,
rounds the curve of
Starr King into Geary,
stalking an unknown synthesis.

Between Turk and Hyde
he envisions a new edifice,
obliging to reason but
uncluttered by context.
A thing to be built
   in this our time
before a lesser edifice
defines tomorrow by default.

He pauses at the juncture
of Post and O'Farrell,
relieves himself against
a sky-blue building,
then chases his tail till
he blurs and dissolves
down a whirling tunnel of time.

The quick red dog jumps over
a crazy black derelict,

seeking a new foundation
beyond desperation,
beyond supplication,
beyond extrapolation.
A new basis for significance.
A place of covenant and exaltation,
floating in the fantastical,
grounded on pylons
of absolute potential,
spanning San Francisco
with a largeness like song.

Ornamental cherries blossom
south of Market as a
red dog converges with Folsom
on Decoration Day,
chased by demons that
he cannot comprehend
until a silent tide of light
befriends him and
delivers him from clatter.

The ghost of Coltrane blows
an alleyway of sunshine
through sophisticated chatter
of ecstatic demi-monde,
through a filter of foglight,

earnest of a new dawning
of concise freedom and
incentive to surpass futile ends.

The red dog lies in a patch
of articulate daylight
inhabiting space and time
with a certain sweet resolve,
inclining an ear to the
shape of sacrificial notes
rising above context:
syntax of a new creation,
revealing new implications
and new resources for
resuscitation of the century
from an order beyond repair.

Head over heels in love,
the red dog catches his tail
and rolls like a fiery wheel
around the corner of 3rd & Howard,
ducking a Greyhound poised
in static flight amid clouds
of diesel fume while
a skid-row ghost town,
phantom pawnshop,
flophouse and tavern beckons

from the reconstructed avenue,
glaring through new paint
with a terrifying scream.

'Cross Market, up Powell he runs,
intersects Grant, leaps Broadway
and reconvenes with Grant
where midnight sunglasses
peer into feathered lights
of a beatific bebop vision
beyond casual compromise.

A magnificent summer replies
with a moment of clear luster,
swinging between cataclysms
to the speech of loud guitars,
streaked gold by a setting sun.

Ancient logic and tarnished synthesis
blend into the sky like twilight
as a red dog stalks the Embarcadero
by first glow of a rising moon,
seeking a sweeter creation
capable of returning tears to eyes
who cried them, innocent of salt,
transmuted into resurrection wine.

Opening Statement

Impromptus of the moment
free but for paper's aqueous flame,
unwilling to go back and undo
what once is said but crash
without explanation into the pool
on enormous bubbles that
pop and spew platitudes
cloud high on a jet of hot steam
trailing tropes and opinions,
thanking the death of stars
for the birth of the worlds.

Give me a hand,
shaped round to
the flat of the sky,
none of it fixed,
none of it firm,
none of it numbered,

the sparrow that barks like a dog,
the horned tusk on the cradle,
the nice lady with pie inviting us
into the glorious gasp of conception.

How can I say that I thought
of you whom I've never met,
cradled your head in the crook

of a shining mechanical arm,
stroked the smoke from your eyes
with a violet linchpin, fattened you
with clusters of grape and cherry,
married you beneath a shower
of tombstones and carried you off
to honeymoon castle pinned to
the lining of a vest of flame?

All you would want and less
than you ever guessed: There are
more of us than you dreamed,
though not all in the same place
at the same time, stretched, instead,
in consecutive lines from first cry
to the last grim rattle of doom,
a million or two blessed by the
hawk in the blue hat appointed
to die by degrees into salt
informing the limbs of Neptune,
the hand that carries the waves
and all who go forth upon toward
home port safe in the eye of God.

With the left hand reason
with the right descry,
speak the warm oil of tongues

to charm the appearance of
fire at the crest of the brow,
a nimbus of sparkling sound.

There is nothing more perfect
or pleasant than that we be here,
ear to ear, later to walk away
able to whistle the tune of it all,
the feeling if not the words which
duck into flame and are gone,

seed of smoke in
the heart of the
flower of the brain,
a light scum of love
that dissolves in the rain.

Wading into the fray
As though possessed
Despite all odds
Bloody but unbowed
Caution to the wind
Not to be nay said
All banners flying
Times without name
Name without number
Written on the wind in ballpoint
I am the gingerbread man
Knock-kneed and trembling
Yellow-bellied and shit scared
  Jumpy as all get-out
    Trembling like a leaf
      Whistling in the dark
    Nervous as ninepins
    One over the elbow
A new way of talking
A new way to talk
A new way of cutting
A new way of cutting through

Do you like it
Do you love it
Do you want it
Do you need it
Will you hug it
Will you feed it,

cut it into thin
strips and eat it?

Flying in the face
Flying in the face
Flying in the face of *danger*

Heedless of harm
Laughing at disaster
Letting chips fall where they may
Without a "by your leave"
Times without name
Name without number
Written on the sky in solvent
I am the gingerbread man
Jittery as all bejeezus
Skittish as a squirrel
  Prudently cautious
    Breaking out in a cold sweat
  Scared of my own shadow
One over the elbow
A new way of talking
A new way to talk
A new way of cutting
A new way of cutting through

Do you fight it
Do you fear it
Do you taste it
Do you hear it

Do you walk up
and rub noses
or just turn
the hose on it?

Flying in the face
Flying in the face
Flying in the face of danger

Reckless in abandon
Sheer force of will
Without regard to life or limb
Nor any backward glance
Dauntless, undeniable
Indomitable strength of purpose
Times without name
Name without number
on the sky in stars written
on the skin in scars
I am the gingerbread man
Lacking intestinal fortitude
  Spineless, frightened out of my wits
    A yellow streak down my back
      Grinning like a shit-eating dog
    Lily-livered with tail
  between legs, cold feet
Heart in my throat
One over the elbow
A new way of talking

A new way to talk
A new way of cutting
A new way of cutting through

I am the gingerbread man
Times without name
Name without number
This is a gingerbread angel
From over the bright blue boom
Flying down to feast on my
Peppermint eyes and pluck
The raisins from my smile.

Names worth dropping
Names in vain
Names to be reckoned with
Forms of address
for the formless
Nomenclature
Omenclature
Womanclature
Euphemism
Newphemism
Ephemerism
Alias the Nameless

This name of mine
This name of yours

I do not paint
I do not dance
I do not dream
I do not think
I do not take
I do not give
I do not light
I do not burn
I do not stare
I do not blink
I do not sleep
I do not wake
I do not live
I do not perish

Flying into the teeth
With feckless mettle
Daring the Devil
Lashed to the mast
With full might and main
I am my name

My name is the name
that when you call it
    I come.
My name and I
answer to anything.

Preserpie & Senti Yagoya

Preserpie & Senti Yagoya
squander the fat purses
of Dismus & Dythimus
on a sordid assortment of
pleasant peasant blouses

then sit by a bank
of the roaring Oreo
trimming a rowboat
with flax & tallow
under a Rolex moon.

Naked to the navel
Ignio Yatayanga
squats in the bushes
wondering: if the gold
screw in his belly
were to be turned
would his ass fall off?

The reason for thunder
with no lightning or rain
could only be blows of
the hammers of elves
says Preserpie to Senti
Yagoya whose eyes
are blue as the milk of
wolves in the wild wood.

■

Dismus offers a stack of
silver coins to a jukebox set
in the trunk of a melon tree,
   containing only
the Songs of Solomon
set in three-quarter time,
played on steam organ
and sung by the sisters
of Immaculate Conception

while Dythimus touches a match
to the thatch of his roof
& sings by its light to the
slight tones of a pocket guitar:

A thousand miles I came
to hear a bear play violin.
The bear played violin,
not very well, but better
than you expect from a bear.

Preserpie & Senti Yagoya
return to the feast of fire
with twelve silver whistles
& a dozen tuned lips to
play them—all which is not
music is fed to the flame.

Exact Birds

Regarding (regarding)
the touted possibilities
of infinity, specifically:
the statistical inevitability
of Shakespeare, the Manhattan
phone directory & the Bible . . .

something in me says
a hundred monkeys,
given eternity,
could not change
a typewriter ribbon.

In service of a
sense of shining,
we dine at six sharp
Take on substance.
Flesh out as they say.

Served moments
after plucking,
garnished only
with appetite, we
of the Ria Rialta
top cabin crew,
plunge knives
in our lives to

improve flavor,
chefs unto death.

Love knows
no such hunger.
We are imported.

Is that a tomcat
rifling the trash
or is it my death
in the darkness
rattling the cans?

Demons or the
neighbor's dog?

—investigation not
a fit response—

Birds make no milk,
the exact birds
as make no cream.

Jaaz #3

Stan Getz and Bill Evans
got lost in a Moroccoan bazaar
back in 1960. They were forced
to live on goat flesh until both
grew horns and small beards.
This may not seem likely
on the face of it nor is there
any moral to be gleaned
except that things are
known to happen sometimes
that never happened before.

Sonny Rollins on the other hand
spent a good part of the sixties
in the woodshed, forsaking
stage and studio altogether,
because someone happened to say
there are only 32 viable notes
on the saxophone and Sonny
was perfectly sure there were
35 although two were elusive
and the third required
perfect serenity but tended
to play itself without
necessity for fingering
if pursued with the whole
heart, mind and soul. This
he did and one may suppose

discovered the note but, if so,
he never played it in public
because stepping outside those
32 viable notes something
tended to emerge which was
not exactly jazz and therefore
not really his bag—

There was this dedicated trumpeter
named Rudy who used to hang with
the same crowd I did in the early '60s.
He would not adhere to the changes
of any impromptu band that gathered
but commenced to blow just as the
spirit moved him taking maybe
24 bars for a 16-bar solo
and causing controversy
amongst those who felt
tight structure was
prerequisite for proper
taking of liberties. Let's just
say he had his own internal
clock and intonation was
not his strong point . . .
Anyway Rudy sidled up to Miles
between sets at the Blackhawk,
blowing cold spit out of his valves
and said "Man you want to

do somethin' together?" and
Miles said "Whatdya wanta
do baby, fuck?" I think this may
have been what broke the man
because he disappeared to
the East Coast and was last seen
by Marty's brother Bobby around '69
in Central Park way late at night
carrying a broken fishing pole.

This was all we heard and
could mean a number of things.
I mean I don't expect he's
still there although the last
you hear of somebody is where
they live forever in your mind
and that's a sadness we accumulate
which has nothing to do with jazz per se.

All roads lead
to the tabletop,
the long board
of locking leaves,
altar of appetite.
Vital as it may
sometimes seem
to distinguish crepe
from flapjacks,
remember: A
menu is not a map.

Feed rather
upon glass fruit,
upon the shine,
the shadow,
or tint of the
glittering pear,
gloss of the
mineral grape,
flesh tone of
amethyst apple
with pits of pearl.

Is it by how
white sun
on fleck tide
rehearses

unfaceted
diamonds
yet to be
found in
critical
snow fields
of blank earth?

Is it by tying
a loose loop
'round the neck
of a stream
& tugging
firmly but
gently until
its tendency to
meander gives
way to a more
linear flow?

If it is our
lot to be ill,
let us be ill
with appetite,
ill to the Blue
Heart of God,
from
the gash

between
ourselves
& eternity.

A place with
numerous roses
is not the place
to speak of roses.
Here alone,
in barren soil
of sand & thorn
do they ghost into
flawlessness
without distraction
of perfume.

Wm. James sat
at table one night,
long after supper,
blessed by a mood
of profound peace,
culmination &
utter satisfaction
until he noticed
something invisible
& menacing in the
corner of the room,

whereupon
he fell into a
state of abject
depression
in which
he remained
submerged
for a period
of two years.
Satisfaction
ruins appetite.

Appetite ruins satisfaction ?

It seems we
must learn to
value the place
of becoming;
the almost but
never quite—
the sense of
· impending as
opposed to the
consummation
of any desire.

World? World
is a way
of looking,
matrix for

raw force
of hunger.
Grass grows
regardless
& sidewalks
care little
who walks them.

What of it?
All seasons
are Spring
in some clime;
not all water
is blue but
song bursts
free of polarity
& the one
can indeed
become the many.

An eagle circles
the ceiling of
this small room
& her wings
whisper as she
brushes the
four corners in

a single sweep.
My cup is
unclouded—
I drink.

Poets on poets writing on
black balloons in the dark
with pencils of light
Poets sweeping the stairs
of syntax with red brooms
and mops of human hair
Poets in white face crashed
in a bird cage awaiting
the call of the catman
Poets with poorboys burning
a festive tire for heat near
Town's End on Christmas Eve

To sink is to swim
if to swim is to fly
is to fly is to fly
in the manner of Irving
black poet of gloom
who genuinely jumped
the Golden Gate
carrying roses in '65
in order to survive—
Foghorns tell his tale

Candles of the coronation
Torchlight of the Sun's corona
grant us sweet song of passage

Poets sworn to the breath
and genius of coincidence
leaving lines as they lay
Poets with word processors
performing infinite revision
approximating spontaneity
Poets listing flat perceptics
in concrete cadenzas
eliciting the music of matter
Poets performing subluxory
transection upon the lungs
and the liver of language

There is meat in the
skin of the fleece
of the sacrifice/
shank, chop
& a rack of rib
but the portion
consigned to smoke
for the nostrils of God
feeds only the worm
at the root of the word

Blood of the coronation
Torchlight of the corona
grant swift song in passing

Poets on poets become Catholic
or High Anglican at the
apex of agnostic careers
Poets in Tantric ecstasy
blowing blue steam out
of the top of the skull
Poets collecting trading cards
of oriental deities, chewing
the tough bubble gum of Dharmakaya
Poets with Ouija boards
converting subtext of the soul
into apodictic synecdoche

All of this dies
None of this dies,
returns full-blown
as though never
said before; as though
controversy had
little or nothing to say
except why nobody
cares much for poetry
except poets and
owners of offset presses

Blood of the coronation
Floodlight of the corona
suffer kind songs of passage

■

Poets on poets obeying the dictum
to make it new while finding
no ideas but in things
Poets become other than poets
by assiduous application
of structural linguistic theory
Poets born less than poets
becoming poets because
a poet is something to be
Poets who are only poets
rising on wings of Ezra where
weight of air cannot bear them

Once it was Heaven
Once it was hot
high sweaty joy
and celebration
in the English dep't
well into Summer
preceding redolent Fall
till Winter came
rescinding the
free rent of the sun

Milk of the coronation
Torch song of the corona
lend us sweet light of passage

■

Poets exercising seven
types of ambiguity
in dog-feather beds on acid
Poets notorious for
public drunkenness on
major career occasions
Poets boiling water at 4 A.M.
to sterilize pencils before
writing the name of God
Poets tanning skins of
fresh-butchered critics to write
Fuck You in brush calligraphy

Paper is cheap
The heart and pencil
perform as well
for you as another
but consider
what it portends
to tell others whom
you do not know
the whimsies of your soul
in a public fashion

Mud of the coronation
Fell light of the corona
give us a serious song

■

Poets who subtract all but
the most pregnant words in
quest of ultimate density
Poets employing only
lower case *i* as
advertisement of humility
Poets who refuse to use
I at all yet speak
of themselves alone
Poets who salt their song
with numerous *I*'s yet
seem to possess none

How can we help
believe in our own,
considering what
we have been
and conspire to be,
full of a fine fury
tempered by time
and circumstance
into exquisite anger
weaponed with words?

Bonfires of the coronation
Flares of the Sun's corona
Rouse us to song in passage

■

Poets who lose change in
the gutter and try to fish
it out with gum on a string
      —complaining of
Poets who believe God speaks
in dactyls and consider
the practice of poetry prayer
      —complaining of
Poets who serve it up
by the pound admitting
it's all a crock and so what?
      —complaining of
Poets in bathrobes fencing
with cardboard tubes
Easter Sunday on the moon

risen . . . it is risen
full on the face of
Balboa's Pacific
tugging the waves
by neckties of froth
twice reflected light
lending sheen to
candescent roar,
throat of the sea
wide open to the sky

Candles of the coronation
Torchlight of the Sun's corona
grant us sweet song of passage
and a tongue of swords to explode
the pus sac of deep profanity

Trapping a Muse

Go for it go under
make your way back
recall what you
went for first
decided to get—got,
declined to keep
woke up on a bus
saw the place go by
and kept riding.

Written in rope 'round
the neck of the famine
"this my own,
my native land,
this my own countree"
men in overcoats
bearing a pall in the rain,
I and not I equally
at ease within the shroud.

How a mild breeze
can shut a door so that
you look up wondering
what she wants of you:
nothing and everything.
Look to your lines
and ignore the source.

A ghost for all seasons,
stroking the nape of
the neck of the moon—
strawberries of Ganymede,
the blood oranges
of Gethsemane;
the dates of Amon Ra.

Sparks of fluttering rings
as she shows the
shape of the smoke;
the smooth sides of the flame.

Useless to imitate
when the thing itself
is far from outstanding.
        This is the
Age of Understanding.
Before it the Age of Marvels.
Before it the Age of Belief,
the flow of the hair
on the scalp of the skull . . .
the beach in the sun of
sea-salt winter—rage
with runes in the
dark of the parking lot.
Metanoia: fear of avenging angels.

Black Sunflower

Depression expression
dangerous not to—
ink gives out
as I start to write—
switch to pencil
which fades from
the page given time.

Date. Why date?
It's the same time
only later. Fade.
The 4 o'clock
pulls out about
one minute to 3
due to daylight savings
and a slow watch.

Didn't want to
go anyway.
Probably a sign.
Yeah, why not?

Remember to number.
What by how
subtracted from why
leaves a remainder
of one. Bye.

Toad in Love

With nothing but quicksilver
sand and salt of the
marsh to tread upon,
where to go when eagles,
stuck by the wing tips to
flypaper coils, remind you
that clocks tell time in the abstract:
the full body blow of the hours
leaves blood on the lips of the soul
bespoken under aegis of
double-dense hearts
betrothed in corkscrew shadows,
a far fall from the Seraphim
genius for love everlasting.

What we have is
what we may lose
by valuing something
we believe to be higher
abjuring love in the dirt
with a ham sandwich
and a sackful of twins . . .

Easy for angels who are
constructed of love, tapped
into the Great Niagara with
perfectly lovely eyes pouring
perfectly lovely light across

perfectly lovely skies,
perfect arch of brow above
strikingly chiseled chins.

We, graveward bound,
have more need of love
than those who have
no bitch with the ultimately
augmented tits of eternity.

Our demise, small as our love,
brittle and flint flaked
as Medusa's dandruff,
is all the more for what it is not,
biologic and brusque,
wearing a snap-brim hat,
tightfisted and treacherous,
contained under such
impossible conditions that
our sheer perversity in
daring to love at all declares
us worthy to stand toe to toe
and slug it out with angels,
trading singing commercials
for hymns of the empyrean,
vision tuned to the faraway
spark of stars more truly
than any given leave to steep
in holy fire or sing within.

■

Starlight come a trillion
miles to sting us leaves
instead a bile of years
spread thin as salt upon
black unleavened bread.

The lingua franca of the sun,
strains of static rhapsody,
cause all yet to be spoken
to appear already said, yet
nothing but inflection makes
one statement to be so and
another to arrive born dead.

Love begins to be uttered
but cannot finally be told:
escapes from the far stroke
of an eyelid to become,
in its own turn, flame,
by which light we learn
that to love is to burn,
return to naked elements
transparent as the ash of snow
born on our own breath
by our own true wind.

The Pool

A look into the pool
shows the face
has not formed
enough to display
features it will
in time contain

your private life and
your private thoughts
all that stands between
you and that face
informing the pool
without permission

the pool is real
though in doubt;
isn't particularly
a metaphor though
it plays like one

being modern you
want to know what
the text is hiding,
what really informs it
which is expected
to be pretty basic
and expectation
is hard to confound

■
when a certain
open-endedness
seems the hallmark
of authenticity,
more a way of
looking at things
than a way
of concluding them

the full cipher
will not be written
since new encoding
is generated in
the solving of it

Sentinel

First Watch

Black to the west,
pearl at the edges,
face full of eyes,
red at the cuff,
my tower of bones
blooding the height
crosswise to the sea
invites the seed to
a telling of dream:

milk of the musk ox
curdled in brandy,
coded and bound to
coinage of fire struck
in likeness of flesh,

mutations of waves
chatter from the
mouths of goblins
biting off bits of wind
and speaking them.

Indifferent rhetoric,
proficiently uttered,
nothing to challenge

the rational—this is
their code and curse.

I observe them from
my tower beside the sea,
call each by name:
the one called Many
and the many called One.
None stands beside me.

My charge lies
in accepting the
evidence of my eyes.
I stand where I stand,
speak as I speak,
take nothing for granted,

all open to doubt,
evidence of eyes
notwithstanding—yet
I do not disbelieve that
things are as they seem,
though in another place
they would seem otherwise.

Not to seem to say
yet to have said: this
is the measure of saying—

■

to encompass without
comprehension,
obeisance made to the
fact that words belong
to the element of air,
that is the art of hearing.

My report is chiseled
in rock; let not its
weight in stone refute
the lightness of its aim,
which is that of music—
yet it will not be music.

Second Watch

A stem twists in my hand,
seeking after its flower but
the flower knows not the stem,
acknowledges no kinship
to the stalk of its arising.

I have a message: Beware!
The stem knows not the root
and the flower presents no seed.

Yet there is perfume in the air
of a phantom blossom blooming.

This is not the Sentinel's
doing; nor was it due to
the council of the crow
that it should be so.
Strange things are brewing.
They will need attending.

The Sentinel calls
the tower to him.
The tower is his song
and enfolds him.

Mystery and reluctance
form concentric rings,
red to umber along
the horizon of such music
as is heard in troubled sleep.

I spy with my brass eye
three stragglers
keeping to the shadow
of a cloud which seems
to travel at their pace.

My challenge to them
is met with insolence.
No reason to detain them.
The only danger they
offer is to one another.
It is the *quiet ones* . . .
those who respond to
challenge and counter-
challenge in all respects
correctly—who seek
to pass unnoticed—
those *meticulous ones*,
who must be detained
and made to answer
pointless questions
till their logic fails them.

Crafting my report,
words come with
annoying fluency
in images not
necessarily of my choosing;

The gods in the apple tree
hold court with the crow.
A girl with a guitar sits
beside the city gate mending
a broken string with twined

filiments of her own hair
then strums a minor chord
raising her voice in mild words
forever stripped of innocence.

A stick snaps in
the berry brush—
noted in my chronicle.

Three stragglers and
a snapping stick—things
have been lively this watch.

What is seen
matters less
than what is said
if it be precisely told.

Third Watch

There is a language which
is spoken, and it has its use
but one does not drive nails
with the flat of the hand.
There is a language by which
stories are told and it has
its use but one does not

poke coals with the eye.
There is a language suitable
for song, its edges smooth
as the face of a coin but
one does not hone knives
on the soft parts of the body.

There is a language
of earth and sky
that inhabits sleep,
of emerald pearls
and black rubies
which seed the soil
to put forth
a transparent flower
of whose loveliness
no song may yet be sung.
Invisibility is its essence;
fragrance has it none.

There are grateful places
where hearts tune to the
resonance of the soul
and healing streams
but we have need
of dangerous dreams.

Fourth Watch

The girl beside the gate
has come again today.
The song she plucks on
the string of her hair
disturbs the wind—
she sings of a still place
where breezes are born dead.

Deeper than marrow,
pain of the terminal
wound risen to full
flower of bruise
after exhausting
all potential for
damage beneath the skin . . .

Out of her mouth blooms
a rare transparent flower
which flows like silk
down the face of her body.

Only the most fluently
adaptable scheme
could hope to apply
a layer of lyric without
intruding on the sound,

fuse the intent and
collapse the structure
into harmless song.

Forbidden entry into
the phantom flower
there's nothing to
be lost in assuming
it makes no difference.

If it is not so,
it must be made
to seem so
and in seeming
come to pass.

Fifth Watch

Jealousy—that things
appear to exist as objects
while I am simply a subject.

Consternation—that
others should know
what they know
by right of birth
while I struggle from

conception to conclusion
knowing less of
what I seem to know
than what I say.

Suspicion—that my
grief is not so noble
as the grief of
the deeply ensouled
who face ruin without
the comfort of delusion.

Fear—that the pool of my
sorrow is so shallow
a moderate day's warmth
will dissipate the flood
tide of my sympathies.

I do not know if a tree
remains a tree when
I turn toward a cloud—
nor if my love is love
or infatuation of the eye
with the bright gilding
of the heart's foundation
by whose inexact light
I happen to see another.

Sixth Watch

The blind heart I behold
reaches across to me;
the fabled lungfish
whoring the stony beach
unfolds a horizon
inloaded with cargo,
infiltrates the springs
of the bed where
children are conceived.

These children are
born bouncing,
fall to the floor like
India rubber balls
and roll as far from
home as the spirit of
the wind commands.
Their cribs yawn wide
producing sometimes
a changeling, sometimes
the wing of a moth or
the feather of some
unseasonable bird as
token that the *other*
mother claimed them.

No more cherries
out of thin air—
the Magus who
produced them has
vanished in the mirror
leaving a dark wound
in the glass from
sudden absence of reflection.

Only in the body of another
does the certainty of freedom
digress into sheer ideal,
bled white by leeches of light.

Interlude

*(words written in his journal
while the Sentinel sleeps)*

Rotten with confidence
the Sentinel dozes in his
shoddy cardboard tower
dreaming of a seashore
strewn with the shells
of calcified redeemers—
hold one to your ear to hear
prophecy in the voice of waves.

He fails, as all must fail,
his self-appointed charge:
to see what's before him,
that alone, unclouded
by desire or concept.

We three, who seem
to him stragglers,
are concept incarnate
fueled by desire—
we three with angels
in our pockets pulling
a cloud by a kite string—
we whose powers
of observation are
focused by the purity
of our intention to
speak only to angels
in prime numbers.
Once inside the gates
we will release them.

By the time he learns
who passed beneath
his nose unheeded,
the angels will have
done their damage,
the snap of the stick in
the brush being only

the faint echo of the
end of the world the
Sentinel seeks to prolong.

The angels will do nothing
but shine in the corners
in radiant absence of action.

By degrees perfect
peace will descend
upon the city until
it will seem it has
always been so.

This is the possibility
the Sentinel selected
himself to guard against:
insufferable satisfaction,
stagnating lack of contention.

Why do we bring such
a treacherous gift? Are
we devils? Far from it.
We are agents of completion.

It is to strike flint to
the consecrated fuel
awaiting combustion;

to ignite the first spark
of all consuming light.
Flame alone frees!

The Sentinel himself
may keep his watch,
confined to his wall by
misunderstanding
of the force he opposes;
crafting reports destined
to go unread but over
which, knowing this,
he will take more pain
as evidence to himself
of his purity of dedication.
Did he but know his own
utility to the angels whom
he sets himself against,
he would cast his spyglass
into the sea in sorrow.
Without him we could
not ignite our holy fire.
He is the sulfurous tip
of our quicksilver match.

When our work is complete
and peace settles in waves
lapping his tower struts

with monotonous precision,
he will lift his clutching eyes
to the shifting conformations
of the sky in search of change;
there will be nothing here to see.

The Last Watch

Trapped in my tower
with no mission but
to sound the bell
tolling the hours
of my captivity,
I survey clouds
and calculate the tide.

Stone axman among
petrified trees, I hear
the seasons shout
farewell in passing,
returning before their
echo is diminished,
years revising the contours
of hill and stream
at astonishing speed.

Spyglass claimed by the sea,
I spend my nights in
naked eye astronomy;
my days staring at the
selfsame sky occluded
by the twinkle of the sun.

I am the witness of
minor variation: no
two sighs of discontent
are identical in cause.

Yet there is value in
seeing things as they
present themselves,
assuming no more
than what they appear
most nakedly to be:
stone lion in the sand
with the face of a man
a simple statue, grand,
but devoid of mystery
as any ring of standing stone
erected to perpetrate the rites
of some who feared the sun
might fail to rise without them.

Beyond the voluptuous
self-consuming vortex
that winnows out of space
and returns along the
track of its own edges,
defying preposition—
beyond or aside from it,
lies the point of rest
I seek and of which
I cannot be mistaken.

In *seeming*
it must be so,
for seeming
is the substance
of apparency,
its sole mode of being.
There is no other measure.

Where is the place
surrendered to mystery
by innocent credulity?
The still place, sterling bright;
the place that must be so?

There I propose to go
defended against night

by a tender history
of absolute futility.

The people of my city sit
cross-legged, absorbed
in their idea of deity
through which they dart
point-blank into the jaws
of their natural enemy
while I study the mold
on the face of a sickly fruit
or whatever comes to hand.

It is enough to see.
What evades the ear
and makes it blind
is simple to the eye.

I have seen the writing
of the three, addressed
to me—and recognize
the hand in which the words
were written: my own.

What witness can withstand
impeachment by the light?

Since it is so, I do not see
how it could be otherwise.
It is no concern of mine
in what manner I was
self-slated to play the fool
to my own Magus of Thebcs.

It is as it must be,
since I am as I am,
a fact among facts,
a figment of my own
observation, like any other.

If Beauty is to be,
it must root in what
is less than beautiful;
allow itself to sprout
shabby foliage serving
as a rough protective
cover for its sced.

The seed has beauty
to outshine the flower.

Let the seed be delivercd
intact, sound in husk
and germ—then all

is accomplished
which has been appointed.

This is my full report,
respectfully submitted
to the seed who knows
those things implicitly
which I suspect in part,
my only business being
to say what I have seen
and then be silent.

Pride of Bone

A sackful of sighs—
Places the Soul
felt her beginnings
then was forced
to forsake in her
steady refusal to
linger, however
chaste or blessed
the temperature
of desire, however
innocent the light.

Soul is the
Pride of Bone.
It has no other.

Irrecoverable,
except to say
something of it,
how it seemed;
what it could
seem to become
by being seen
in a different light.

The past alone changes.

Said time is
tolerable,

time unsaid
is dying.

Soul is the
Pride of Bone.
It has no other.

We cannot learn
from the past;
we *are* the past.

Have we lost
our magic?
Another magic
is unfolding.

In this hand
nothing,
in that hand
nothing—

Look—
a seed!

Soul is the
Pride of Bone.
It has no other.

Rain in a Courtyard

. . . for Rick Griffin

mood struck
fog flowers,
wind sculpt
flatland of
comet rock,
lesser jewels,
delphinium
& slag with
no end rhyme
waking into
bright rooms
yawning with
morning sun
in blue rain

fed on recipes
& schooled
on symbol
summoned
for its own
striking sake,
all the old
expansions
gathered in
a tight fist
to shake at
the mindless
song of stars,
cloud fleece,

smiling sun &
wistful waves

the gods of
this world
offer
rainbows
as recompense
for sloppy skies

they also silence
whom they love,
knowing how
there's no
percentage in it;
how none of
it's worth
breaking a heart for.

Not that
this was
always so.

In the tree
a half pecked
persimmon,
      in the
courtyard
   rain.

Sonnets in Stone

Man on a marble lawn looks up at
singing of sorts shading into murmur,
wind folded back on itself exhausted,
bridges spanning broad-breasted water
with regular swells something like song.

City of stone: stone streets, stone houses,
stone dogs barking stone warning at stone
cats in lava trees climbing the sky like
a leprous mother cobbled in darkness,
pit of the earth sprung sulfurous wind.

Curl and retract, thistledown returning
to the bud of its birth, to the groin of earth
descended to the crucible where dozing
eddies of whirlwind sculpt the lava into
eyes sunk in sockets of coal dreaming

things as small as moons gleaned from
rivers of silky black magma, the throat
of every star. Listen, it said, suppose I
began as not more than a slight sighing,
would you like to try to learn to love it?

Listen, she said, suppose a winter of nursing
a child on fire and lye while storms spew
out of volcanoes, a portion of the foundation

erupting to revive the deflated wind,
its groaning in caverns mournfully shrill,

primitive with punctuation, grieving for
long-lost loves of the future, restless and
ill-amused, a bearded crone shattering
hearts yet to be born, sucking the elements
out of the stones, snatching sparks between

sharp fingers and squeezing them into stars,
sounding the cry, the fire song, the clatter
of hell through the veins of basalt and iron,
rage become stone become ice become voice
become light become rain become wind,

listen, she said, sleek, sudden and gowned,
stepping from the craterous mound chaste
as bituminous clay: if I let it begin slowly
and we wind our way there by degrees,
how unwilling can you be to come with me?

Seven Trials

drowsing
lips shaped to the
curve of the cup

suddenly awake
running like hell
but it's gone

seems dangerous
to begin again
but what have you?

after a few weeks
it's like starting over
first things first

don't have time
don't have patience
don't have nerve

hard not to make
more of it than it is
whatever it is

the difference shown
in an inclination
of the head—slight

anger
suspicion
disdain—desire

You have to find
something else to want,
against all inclination

trespass at leisure
love has better things
to do than beware

Dew on the Daisy

Well, it's been swell and
the dew is on the daisy—
or is the daisy on the dew?

A cat's meow hangs
on the bark of a dogwood
where thistles glisten.

All day to write it down
but long about eve it
didn't need to be said.

I said it anyway out
of desperation,
self-centered and blue,

a rude departure
from an old
line of attack,

but who can keep
that up without
alerting the clouds?

Could make what
isn't needed into
what is cared for

because odds are
it's necessary to
care for something

more than it may
ever care for you
if only to get even

with whatever
forces one into
such a position.

Rimbaud at Twenty

Clearing dead ash
from the iron grate
with a penpoint so
the stove can breathe,
make quick tinder
of vision to heat the
room if not my heart.

Tomorrow I leave
France and the
unwanted love
of idiots I can
no longer tolerate.

I saw as I spoke
and speak no more;
wish only to see
as other men see
who find little to say.

Embracing flame
with flesh, I am
the son of bone
who has no mother.

There's bone in beauty
but no beauty in bone.
Only steadfast utility.

■

I was never mad.
Deranged,
delirious,
daring—but
never insane,
unless at long last,

but this I know:
There is no
satisfaction
in high Hell
or the Angels—
Pursuit is all.

After a night's
chase I woke
with testimony
in hand, no idea
how it got there.
My own and
not my own,
a stranger's notes
in my very hand.

The part that
clung catlike
to dry dock in

drunken seas—
writing rather
than allowing
me to drown
in raw glory of
vision's blood—
argues my sanity;

the bitch of a poet
who bartered my
lucid & perfectly
transparent death
for delicate domes
and angular words
        is no more!
I killed her with
my own hands
and now I am
one alone,
without content.

Brother of an
only child
born an orphan.

Now I follow
a slender, less
austere death
to a tropic with

no relation to this
world where I
failed my doom,
pleasured myself
as it bleached my
blood to a thin
white milky sap.

Now others
attempt to
become what
I discard like
a leprous ear.
The pitch of
their fever
is the illness
of an hour.

Seeking strange
hybrids of glory
where there is
only humiliation,
they covet the
tongue I pulled
from my throat
tossed in the alley
for dogs to contest.

The choice to be
as I have been
was never mine;
a colloquy of spirits
cast lots for the
stinking rag
that was my soul.
My corpse walks
lighter without it.

I seek climes with
gods whose names
I shall not study
to learn; where
my old familiars
no longer infest—

neither the demons of
Heaven nor those of Hell.

How We Love

Because we love
  what we love
  in the *way* we love,

    not as we
  should love

we love completely
  or not at all

    —other than that
  we study Spanish
    in night school

and learn to forgive those
who seem to be in love
  when we are not
  and do not beg our pardon.

Salutation

When first you
came to me
I thought your
hat was part
of your head.

Only when you
removed it did
I realize that
the love in
my heart was
the only polite
form of address.

Consultation

Swell to see you
between lives
face to face with
so little to say,

you in your
red blouse,
waving from
a red window

set against
a red sky
with scant
red clouds.

Your thoughts
are thinner;
you must be
thinking less.

How do they
light fires in
a world with
no wood—

how do they
quench thirst

in a world
without wine?

It's too chilly
to stand here
facing away
from the sun,

would it help to
walk around or
is this coolness
a characteristic?

So you're
hanging
out with
dead men?

What other
  kind are there?
Don't recede,
  I'm only joking.

Is it true you
wipe your
butts with
Shakespeare?

Or that nothing
worth saying has
ever been said?
Astounding.

I'm not ready
to be dead if
this is what
it amounts to—

but it's nice
to see you in
hopeful colors
all the same.

Like music, you give
every appearance
of significance while
saying nothing.

Omnia Praeclara Rara

It does no harm to
add the water hot
It does no harm at all

Excellence being rare,
one stands for many,
declining to beg
among flame for cinders,

and though the world
be starved for song,
renounce melody to
inspect the heart of words

It does some harm
to add the water cold—
but less than adding none

Seed of the sapling
pale and believing
listen to the thorn
put forth singing,
bough and branch of
flowering aspidistra
going dong ding in
a sky-tinted frieze of
gasping silver fishes

The tiresome young and
the tiresome old . . .
we are tiresome people
who go upright on two legs

Nothing more tiresome
than our words unless
our music—tiresome
for a tiresome age—
tired born and tired
to employ the grave

Let me climb, Rapunzel,
see oh see you wear your
apron low below the knees
and 20 feet of golden braid

How may rack of lamb
be mated in a sequel
to the bone of dream?

Add the water
hot or cold, it
does no harm
to broth of stone

Storm-enshrined mountain
darker than feeling,

the blistering horn,
the blood bell ringing,
sundown's swallow
sings in the branch
muted by rain from
clouds crushed to fit
her quick lowering sky

Cocktails With Hindemith

Broken by dogs
Arrested in form
The fast flying ball,
the ball in the wall,
caught and returned
with a flick of the heart,
claims against one
claims against all
claims against one and all
because wanting it done

Wanting it done now
Most sparkable flow
Sense of amazement
Breath of the breath
Flame of the flame
filed in ivory fiddles
roused out of early slumber
Response of the law
to a part of the body
reserved for carrying coins

The word is a loose flame
The sense must be
put into it like a peach
shoved into a peach pit;
anything can be added

to disguise the center
but the fact of the tilt
can be construed from
the angle of the axis

What may be seen to be climbing
is less than an ivy but more than
a naked trellis—

You never needed it
You never needed it to carry
You never needed it to carry on
You never needed it to play
touch tackle in the backyard
with Kaufmann's Nietzsche for
your own golden football
You never did—You never did
You never will
and there's an end to it

It's growing now
into a full sense of the
form of its shadow,
fulfilling its format,
assuming its stance,
already the trellis
appears more modest

The word is a loose flame;
the heat of it must be
pried out like a pearl
containing an oyster
containing a shell,
like a bird containing
a nest containing a tree,
like an eye containing a cloud
containing a sky

What we have is intelligence
What we want is simplicity
What we have is a theme in C
What we want is the key of E flat minor
What we have is the voice of reason
What we want is a silent prayer
What we have is a square sun
in square sky with square clouds
because we were not content with
circles, ellipses and spheres . . .

You could say it was aimless,
this refusal to let said be said,
this rebel lightning,
this charmed circle,
this Abba, this Ahba
this Abba Ahbarabaca
and other Aberacadaberas

this Sator, Arepo, Tenet, Opera, Rotas
this absolution without revelation
which *is* tyranny,
this tar paper block with
the glass dome reflecting
cocktails by starlight,
Hindemith on player piano,
lips in the dewdrop shadows,
you could say it was aimless,
first, last and always—you
could say so and consider it said.

Something is lengthening.
Something is long. Is it
a sunset or a song? If a sunset,
why does it not sink and if
a song, why is there no melody?
Maybe it's whatever it could be
to serve some purpose which
is less than communication
but more than a vow of silence.

Something is lengthening.
Something is long. Is it
fact or a fiction concerns us
or merely a motion where motion
was not thought possible?

Something is lengthening.
Something is long—could
it be love charring a cinder
through the heart of the candlewick?

Blue is to blue as to spin is to spin
in identical orbits 'round one and
the same sun, rising and falling
in vino veritas over the glad hum
of the hearth of incandescent earth,
swathed in bright aluminum, sworn
into testimony this morning at six A.M.
with the full force and power of song
in the court of cantata, the antechamber
of saints, spirits and souls seen in the
mirror behind the stairs along with
a full-dress moon in a folding chair.

The word is a loose flame;
we are lanterns with legs
chasing it 'round the lexicon,
seeking reflections of our
inner hearts in *mutatis mundi*,
finding the glaciers of Venus
hiding beneath the porch at dawn
guarded by a dog with a broken leg.

Blue Moon Alley

Why do I think
I remember you
by another name
I either heard
or somehow knew

which may not
be memory at all
but some trick
of association,
summoned by

the grave shading
turning into dense
purple brooding in
this darkened room
opening on waves

where the two of us,
out of a limited
number of possible
combinations, were
gifted to be born

by circumstance
or coincidence
more collusive

than chance
or probability

We read & talk
as stars fail &
gravity traps
the beams of
collapsing suns.

Anonymously kindled,
this bleak uneven light
is sufficient to read
the small inscriptions
of joy that sustain us.

The New Jungle

A good day is
a day nobody
stayed away
but nobody came

The New Jungle,
present & perfect,
no memory of
being otherwise,
invincibly green

Terra Cognita
before love was
given a word to
isolate it from
a flight of birds
turning *flock left*
in rarified light
as of one mind

New Jungle,
the Old Earth

water of separation

corrective press
of regarding waves

throat and heart
desiring touch

mouth of the water
lips of the sea

grant it the
thing you are
to enable the
thing you'll be

salt rapture
surrounded

passion seeks
what is likely
to consume it
or it would be
less than love

A good day is
a day someone
was born and
nobody died

How It Really Goes

Having never been
killed before, to my
knowledge, I didn't
know what to expect.
The pain not being
excessive, I was
able to think as they
wheeled me to X-ray
and what I thought
was "this might be it"
and it seemed like
it would be OK, not
as big a deal as I'd
been led to believe.
Possibility of dying
seemed acceptable,
palpably imminent.
What became clear
was that it was not
time—too much
undone—a family,
a new child to raise
and books to write.
So I knew I wouldn't.
Die that is. Not now.
Opportunity passed.
The heart attack was
not one after all, just

my chest kicking back
after cracking a rib
falling off a low roof.
Presented, considered
and rejected: death
as a proposition with
no component of fear.
How else would it be?

Growing

One night with
falling stars
the other man
in the moon
suddenly
rediscovered—

Recognition of
a flavor out of
seventh summer
only to forget
everything we're
made of

Stars, baby

Who made common
cause with the elements?
Called iron his neighbor;
could say of gold:
I knew her as a child.

He is risen!
Holding his breath,
standing quickly
without blacking out,
he glides through

the playground gate
at twilight looking for
empty bottles
he can cash for deposit.

Yagritz

As might a light sleeper
attack autonomous
daylight with blinds

so might Midas
speak his mind
without metaphor
scheming to deny
any substantial song
to the flat horizon
in thought balloons

proud as a pillow
doing soft time
caught out hiding
meats in the attic
bedded in union
divided by twins

stacking black syllabics
point counterpoint to
the crystalline substrate
epitaxic as no other lingo

climbing a laddered seam
in a short shift intent
on southern exposure

Georgia inclusive
Florida moreover
Veronica redux
thumbing the leaves of
the Mind's Eye Revue
hewing to no creed
saw Jesus in blender
and fainted

Has this transom
been thank you
more often than
not so much
  or been shaken till
prophecy settled in
fleck foam attesting
to the less than so,
the more than
merely nothing

axis of no axis
forever an organ
unclear as to origin
set   set   set   *Collide*

Pretty red bird
Pretty red bird winging
Pretty red bird winging west

■

Midas with justice might
break into be continued
thanking you dead in
equatorial ink and resign

By the might of what moon
hauling tide to the Urals
by Estonian Steppes
might Midas
lay claim as the
man of loss foretold

Hosanna Forsythia
multiply multiply
incubate ratify
amen to the stars
where no one
is anyone's equal

torn from the end
of the book and
pasted into the preface
laundered in semaphore
corrected in vanishing ink

Not over there
Over here

Voice to voice
Dead center align
Total description
by detailed process
of omission
freighted in index
larded with lightning

One stroke from
absolute precision
it was silence
undeceived them:
the Dickinson daisies
the small boats
the wedding shore
immortal as ice
at the top of the world

mens aeterna est
quatenus res sub
specie aeternitatis

This is to follow
what went before
Let it be given
to the night and
see what thrives

■

Pretty red bird
Pretty red bird winging
Pretty red bird winging west
Away to the west
Away to the west

The translation
least like a lie
is the clearest
misunderstanding
for the moment

neither invention
nor equivocation but
a gift handed down
to the last born by

the child of a child
    who hopes
you might see
that the use of it

is ornamental

and cease mistaking Father
for Olson in Berkeley
hanging on a cross

■

with a fifth of Scotch
where ears have wings
and the wings have flown

Sense of Impending

Something rejoices.
Something rejects.
Something ignores.

With no regard
to legality
Life legislates

against Death.
Civilization
has that purpose.

Death is what
happens to
someone else.

Then you get
nostalgic for it.
Good Old Death

the way it
sweeps away
the sun & stars.

Been party to
the likes before.
Strumpets in

bumping cars,
strip Bingo
at the bazaar,

vertigo without
the luxury of
suitable heights.

No one expects you
to jump over your
elbow for this but

what of the night you
finally understood
your own intentions
and didn't bother
to warn the others?

myself as the type
nor was she inclined
that we first became
who were only mildly

at whatever cost
taken at face value
while others dwell
laughingly over it

sensible compromise
total unless you mean
could not account for
or accept with regret

denying she ever had
nor making allowance
less than scrupulous
or alarmed in retrospect

inaudible reticence
swiftly slammed shut
to hope without trust
otherwise no reaction

flat of a hand to the
slip of a tepid sigh

downside the upshot
declined with regards

stolen in broad sun
wild to the waist in
forcible recognition
slow inch by quick mile

salted strawberries
four to the platter
splashed down with
apple wine & wind

Ration Your Cylinders

Consciousness is a stolen car
Relax into absolute tension
No lights No smile No trial run

Clutch when you shift
It affects the whole
train of transmission
Up is to down as
float is to sink
Ration your cylinders

This is big action
It flows into gear
The wheel turns
of its own volition
The sacred smile
accepts a sandwich

Lack of theme is
the master theme;
absence of item
an item itself

We do not go
so we cannot return
Once we made as if
to go but could not

Once we tried to
return without leaving,
found a message
nailed to our feet:
"Now you know
all about nothing"

O dog of the dump,
the lips are the
heart of the face
What do we have
we did not have before

other than perspective?

Power of Persuasion

How crazy are the crocodiles
in Anna Nealy's cotton crib.
Born Summer to be thus
trading in night skin
suffering solid sense of
corded catastrophe,
braided table leaves and
something about a golden rake
winnowed by force in whose hand?
I don't care. It has been done.

The adventure is ominous
but the hint of freedom
is too fair to behold distant.

All force of reasons concur
that what's to be done
is to be done differently
since what's been done
demands only a sequel.

The original is impressive,
not less so than the copy
scripted in fair hand but
mistakes are a form of creation
and size argues the stakes of inflation.

Fate holds the lease.
Death could intervene.

Understanding that,
the options are easy:

throw crows to the wind
and swallow your trail
one footprint at a time
beginning with the last.

One Day in July

I elect to do nothing but
bask in the symmetry of
one jewel of a day in July,
exalt and cajole it to become
more nearly human, though
human it never was, past
all that though not beyond.

I'll do this until
the bell rings nine then
climb hand over hand
the ladder prepared
westward into night.

Clotilde, it is sunny.
Flowers nod
on skinny vines,
a door of cloud
swings on
hinges of breeze.

So far from harm,
the promise of the
kind of a day it is,
insinuating no sort
of reminder it was
ever otherwise.

I sat here, Sunday as
ever it is, unable to
consolidate the day,
so I thought I'd
speak of it and try
to pry my thought
from its wistful clutches.

Day as day, lengthened
into mid-late afternoon,
attempts to enchant but
I'll be no party to spells.
All spells are spells
of vanishment but one,
the song of the blue veld.

No attempt to use the day,
only to press my will
up and against the perfection
that all too easily baffles
my soul into acquiescence
shrouded in calendars.

Alone for two weeks,
I've tended to gaze
at days slipping by,
making little or no effort
to catch up with them.

Finally, today appears
slowed to my own pace.

I am, after all, Man—
time is *my* invention.
Days are as may be
under the signet
of eternity. I am
going nowhere else.
What are days to me?

Could it be roses
are calling me?
I will feed them
October wine,
clusters of crickets.

I am not the sort
of person flowers
ordinarily speak to,
but in extremity
they are not proud
who tends them.

Should the day deliver
full weight of promise
I won't breakfast till
twilight, full of what

needs to be said about
this particular day
to distinguish it
from a chalk mark
on the wall of a cell,
time served instead
of time serving—
freedom no longer
potential but present,
this and never another.

Wind picks up,
swirls the tops of trees
rousing venom from
flowers that enflame.

I would there were
an Autumn country
where leaves were
ever red and brown,
nearer to Summer
than the Winter edge
of Fall—enduring.

A place between
September and
mid-October cast
in a cool, rational

light reflecting dreads
of Winterfall from
a distance, if at all,
pleasantly ominous
phantoms of the air.

Enough of that.
Circle around
and make of it
something said.
Rise and carry
what song is left
in the afternoon.

A little past six,
the phone pole shadow
has entered the ivy
at an acute angle
to the east window,
more solid to sight
than the sun splintered
stick which casts it.

In this clime dark
will not come
till well after nine.
The day dawdles with
the length of seven

squeezing the juice
of the hour leaving
only the rind.

I think a day like this
is not counted against
accumulated time—
no sense of it passing
but only persisting
through changing light.
A song could be found
here already written—
caught, caged and carted
away to a day far distant
but the inclination is
to let it remain and feed
on the afternoon shadow,
slip away unsung into
some oblique angle of sun.

How much true time
does anyone need
to perform deeds
we feel within us?
A few days suffice
to shape essentials.

But, having time,
a way is found

to spend it:
by defining,
refining,
losing sight,
regaining it,
rethinking,
reworking it into
one or another
borrowed conclusion.

There's no moral
proposition here.
Time, like flowing
shanks of lava, is
anything but moral.

Evening voices settle
in low ranks against
high banked clouds.
Fairness deteriorates
into serviceable gray.
Differing threads
of lateness gather.

Switch on the light
and heat up a can
of soup for supper,
Cream of July with
a sprinkle of pepper.

After my meal,
an unexpected trace
of the song of the day
remains in my bowl
minus its hours.

A pleasant thing to do,
bring this day to you,
Clotilde, like water
in cupped hands,
spilling a few drops.

But now I will end
because it is done.
The last of the light
untangles from sight
like a squashed glove
on the horizon
and now it is night.

An American Adventure

Chapter One:
Novus Ordo Seclorum

There was no time like the time we
thought something was happening
which was not what we thought it was
but might as well have been considering
how little it was anything else.

If what was seen is to be spoken of,
it must be said all in a breath or
it becomes something else: a glyph,
a gloss, a reflection of a vase bearing
an artificial flower on a living stem.

If what's said in a breath isn't
heard in a breath, it was never said
to begin with . . . and if it takes a walk
on the coals to convince you that faith
is more than a metaphor, you've achieved
the most you can expect from a hot foot.

To go back to the beginning,
what did we think it was
leaked out of the sea dream
of our age to swallow us whole
and later spit us up on the very spot
we'd have chosen for ourselves
had we known it existed?

Behold a city half visible along
the cloud line, studded with
faraway spires, domes, turrets
and other paraphernalia with
which deep-seated yearning
tends to outfit a horizon.

A beckoning beam glimmers
across furlongs of pale grain
waving between us and what seems
our individual and collective destiny.

In retrospect it's fruitless to try to determine
if it was simply arrogance compounded
with sensory overload . . . or if we really saw
something else besides, in its true and difficult
form, not always at a distance; something
not generally given to standing still in the
same spot in an attitude of welcoming.

As for entering the cloud-line city,
indistinct memories tell us
we did so, although snapshots
from the era indicate that it
might have been otherwise.

The inch-thick layer of immaculate
shamrock glass which coated the
pavement is shown, in the photo,

to be only unadorned city concrete
and not all that clean.

There is no evidence of spires
and the pack of gangling gawkers
posturing in the foreground—
could that be us?
Time is the great counterfeiter—
it was not like that. I know.
I was there. I remember.

There must have been a particular day
when it became common knowledge
that the dream was over—God knows
the songs were suddenly full of it,
though it was not clear where the
messengers got their information.

That particular news sailed clear
over our heads, immersed in the
so-called dream as we were—
or perhaps it was intercepted at
office level and stuck in a dry file,
labeled something misleading like: *endive*—

Intending to leave the world
a better place than we found it,
a misleadingly innocent trope,
we were eventually forced to

conclude that it had a logic
of its own having only so much
and no more to do with *us*—
although we still harbored
designs on what we refused
to believe it no longer was.

Now is the future past,
the appearance without
the apparatus of power,
the peaceable kingdom of
wide-eyed glaring beasts
frozen into immobility
by a vision too extreme
to fit behind closed lids.

We assess it as though it were
beyond our control but in our hearts
cannot quite manage to believe that.

It seems there's something
we could have done other than
hope for the best and trust that
somebody more responsible would
come along and put it all right.

But nobody came and in the space
of a mere decade, the fabulous city

lay smoking and desolate, the rags
of its ruin unfit for restitching.

It was then that we understood
we were dead . . . but it made
no difference. The object of our
faith still showed its beacon light
despite the condition of the city.

Or was that only the neon sign
of an all-night car wash
flashing through solid
sheets of unremitting rain?
Whatever it was began
to cut off altogether for
a day or two at a time,
growing to weeks and months.
It wasn't sudden. There was
time to get accustomed.
There was time to wonder just
how brightly it ever shined at all.

After a while imagination began
to substitute lights of its own.
But nothing seemed to possess the
steady, mysterious beckoning quality
of the beacon of earlier days,
with its promise of untellable things
soon to be revealed to the joy of all.

Cut to a rattrap stumbled upon
in a trip to the wine rack where
bottles of Thunderbird age in
temperature-controlled darkness,
wine of the stone-eyed goddess
of scrofulus grace, high priestess
of the grass that pushes its way
through the shamrock glass
to reduce it to seedy sidewalks

a trap expanding in size
to the dimensions of fear
baited with the guts of a weasel
and chained to the cellar floor.

Never mind that the trap is
only apparent and the bite of its
imaginary steel on an imaginary
leg yields only imaginary pain,
for which imaginary medicine
·and an imaginary vacation will
generally deal an imaginary cure.
It still can deal imaginary death,
which, as the son of any respectable
Denver bum can tell you is a
fair substitute for the real thing.

■

Meanwhile, stuffing ourselves
with snapshots of steak while
thrumming and nictating over
a salad of stringent mitosis,
open to charges of pandering
with the flat of the hand held
parallel to the sky as though
seeking moisture independent
of the provided cloud system,
offending an angel or two to be
wrestled later, in the privacy
of the skull, the question arises:
Was the faith we had worth saving?
Consider the alternative . . .

searching the skies, the cards,
the gizzards of rats, random
images, modern pop prophecy or
the latest simulacrum of the psyche
for *any* potency willing to present.

Spellbound in a bubble of glass,
warm flesh believes. Garroted,
gelded and clapped in cold irons
or left to compost in some carefully
calculated public perception, one

breath without hesitation suffices
to declare that flesh believes
to the roots of its teeth or dies.

A glyph. A gloss. A post-midnight
resuscitation beneath a weather-beaten
leatherneck of a moon. New Atlantis
rising from a duck pond in the year
of the dogs in red bandannas chasing
Frisbee in the park.

Summing up what it meant but
no longer means to a disenchanted
generation without many illusions
about illusions, proper discretion
lies in not noticing the severed
dog head in the instant pudding.

We need three ears to hear
the belated truth: an extra one
for what was never said.

What is said all in a breath must
be received in a similar way.
What is not heard in one
quick snatch of the earball,
the content of a single breath,
however elongated, is not

heard at all. Reasoned out
or possibly divined, but not heard.

To hear is to forget, for a moment,
all but what is being said.
To forget precedents and
probable antecedents. To
forget who is saying and
who receiving. To listen
is to change places with
an idea, an idiocy, a saxophone,
a prophecy or a proposition.

Search for certainty destroys
any sense of proportion. Kid
starts out eating crayons and
ends up engineering a hostile
takeover of Gerber's.

And meanwhile, there is music . . .
Music is not a substitute for
meaning . . . *it is a replacement!*
Is this dangerous? It would be
if it were not, you know, *music.*

Sometimes it sounds like
bubbling syllables rising
from the scud and garnish

of the deep. A new thought to
be set beside a known one . . .
the unknown always adjacent
to something known.

When what is unknown is set
beside another unknown, any
sensible carnivore becomes wary.
Which is when, out of fear
or simple prudence, we tend
to freeze it, put it on a stick
and call it a popsicle.

It differs from a bicycle in that
it comes in flavors but, naturally,
makes poor transportation.
Really tragically poor.
Lick it if you like but don't
try to drive it to Los Angeles
in under six hours.

Second Movement:
Annuit Cœptis

Besides hogging most of the
mayonnaise, the Beagle Boys
demand the lettuce be cut

into bite-size chunks, assign
unforgiving deadlines and
stick us with promotion
designed to wilt the parsley,
all the time laughing up
their cardigans humming:
I did it my way with yours.

When the contract comes up
for renewal we wonder:
why not cut loose from
the whole avoirdupois, and
open up a salad bar of our own
with only ourselves to answer to?
Hire our own tomato growers,
import avocados from the moon
. . . take bids on the chives . . .

It might work. It should work.
It *will* work. Spruce up the
environment by arranging for
some <u>blues</u> with progressions
modeled on the tesseract to play
over the sound system, feed
rabbits the salad scraps and
teach 'em to lay hard-boiled eggs.
All we need to do is mortgage
our hats and coats which we

don't need anyway because
the summer is endless
and so is the promise of song.

Suddenly the times change
tripping our g-g-g-generation
in midstride. The bottom drops
out of Caesar salad forthwith
as alfalfa sprouts are discovered
to cause mental retardation and
probable damnation in fruit flies.
They'd kick us out of the tossed
green game if they had the option
but are unable to do so because
we can rent out the lettuce shredder
and live off our own endive.

How High the Moon?
High as we can reach on
tiptoe to secure the far end
of a clothesline and hang
our hearts out wet in the rain.
The weather may change,
but who entirely believes that
the wrinkles fall out on their own?

The fact that no one disbelieves
suffices. Repetitive death on the

racks becomes a fact of life but
there seems to be a market for
endive and hard-boiled rabbit eggs
out in the provinces—so we
hook a caboose to the salad train,
restring our nose flutes and practice
making noises like a carrot
to attract what rabbits remain.

There are things we need to know
and that we know we need to know.
Did Hannibal cross the Alps on an
alligator and if so how many brass
coots in a brass-coot tree? Answers
to these and other critical questions
seem to depend, ultimately, on cranking
it out until (or unless) physically restrained.

Uncompromising ridicule from the press
is resolved by forgetting how to read.

Not only what was said but what
wasn't gradually assembles an
audience as confused as we are.
Avenues plainly marked *dead
end* are taken at breakneck speed
without appreciable brakes

although the perception is of
glacially slow movement. One day
it appears we've been here forever.

A glyph. A gloss. A random
motion of microscopic particles
suspended in gas or liquid
caused by impact with molecules
of the surrounding fluid.
Brownian Movement and no mistake.

Parry, thrust, kick off the body
and lick the blade. Stick it, kick it
and lick it. This could be fun were it
not in such deadly earnest. A sense
of adventure infuses failure which
later success can only approximate.

How many glass cats in a glass-cat stew?
Six if you dine at five. Eight if at nine
abiding in cause and consequence by
exercise of free will or some convincing variation
making a <u>virtue of necessity</u> . . .

which turns out to be the
combination to the safe!
How you got it is immaterial
to the contents of the strongbox

which are variously edible
or negotiable for chattels
foreign and domestic, such as
Hegelian head cheese,
Tasmanian rope money,
or the rare blue endive
that grows only on
the dark side of the moon.

Approaching the frontiers of the ocean,
nonswimmers are lashed together
to make a living raft with promise
of being resuscitated with kisses
if they only keep swimming until
they black out. In deeper than we
had no idea and the plain fact was
we'd forgotten how to drown, or,
more to the point, never knew how.

Among things the late '70s has
had it with is shit like the ideals
we are assumed to represent. Our
actual values were probably too
diffuse for reductive consideration,
could even be said to co-opt
certain powers reserved for Church,
State and the Networks, such as
infathomable vagueness and

promiscuous fondness for
gathering large numbers of people
together for purposes not altogether
unrelated to mutual gratification.

Too late to say *sorry*. Sorry only
cuts it with the motherhood crew.
Without apologies, we keep trying to
stick our pig vomit in the ears of the
public just as if nothing has happened,
disregarding the tempo of young America
at work and play and other febrile notions
of progress in the field of demotics.

Problems to do with trust accrue
like spiders behind a dart board.
Wrath of reluctant realization:
where it all comes from
comes from somewhere else
and that somewhere is not here.

After a bout of threatened retirement,
we brush the cobwebs from the pane
of a studio window believed to open on
nightmares, only to find a friendly
gathering of concerned faces pleased
to find everybody isn't dead in there.

And then the light dawns: the
whole implausible coda is not only
strictly necessary but ultimately
capable of withstanding dense
critical scrutiny. It is what it is
and there is nothing else like it.
And it's ours, all ours, *hahahahaha* . . .

Some kind of test has been passed
with no one knowing exactly what
or why. Certain mistakes will not
be made again; fresh mistakes
beckon with perfumed eyes.

Back alive and bleeding from
numerous nonfatal slights,
exponentially increasing throngs
of salad lovers gather to the sound
of the lettuce shredder in full fury,
operating outside its assigned time
slot and into the untended present,
causing a hole in the fabric of continuity
big enough to drive a truck through.

The spires of another day are
finally visible again, still set
firmly on the horizon, though
the beckoning beam no longer

seems to operate . . .
could it be that we've arrived?
Then why are the spires still
at a distance? Because that's
what they are—they're the
faraway spires. That's all.

All of this happens flying
by the seam of your jeans
thinking someone else is dying
when the roses are for you.
Found picking pepper when the
hurricane hit the pepper tree
we suddenly found ourselves
with a *whole load* of pepper;
more pepper than anyone
might have thought. Enough to
make a pepper pie and then some.

Something needed to be said
about it and still does—or
they rip out your gums and
bill you for individual extractions.

To say anything at all, out of the
countless ways things *could*
be said, it's necessary to say
it as it occurs to you, whether
it's worth expressing or not.

■

If it's a thought of your own
and the urge to speak it is strong,
it makes its own reasons
and provides its own context—
so long as it's said in a breath it
will at least have a chance to
get said, from which follows that
it just naturally becomes history,
official or otherwise.

Whether it finally reflects what
you intended to express must
remain a mystery. The context
itself is mute, but it probably
makes little difference *what*
the exact intent, so long as
the initial thrust sufficed
to compensate for a fuel tank
later discovered to be entirely
empty since somewhere shortly
after takeoff time. Thank God no
one thought to check the gauges or
we'd still be back on those alligators
climbing every mountain in search
of a comfortable swamp to decamp.

Meanwhile, a horse, a cow and
3 blind mice are discovered down

in the cornfield shooting high dice
with the corporate kitty . . . merely
strategic problems are minuscule
compared to the weight of this one.
Trust itself has been violated.

Act Three:
Debts Public and Private

If it is to be said it had better
be said all in a breath—the
thing we think we know so
well, yet can rarely remember
to say aloud—believing it's only
because we forget to remember
to say it that it's so rarely articulated . . .
rather than adducing the fact of the matter,
which is that it only exists when
formulated by living breath.

It has to be said before someone
changes the subject forever—and
affirmed with the tacit understanding
that sometimes it's good to be wrong—
not just about details—but—you know
. . . about *everything.*

To be precisely useless has its uses,
reciprocity being what it is and
depending as it damn well does
upon the ability to rip off
a piece of territory and spend
the rest of your life defining it.

Are we talking Rock? Or just
some species of the Roll?
In deference to the nonpresenting
metaphor, it becomes wonderfully
apparent that when you have
nothing to add to what you've
already said you shut up or
suffer the consequences.

Seven years of silence drives
inarticulation to a new high
but the breath is not abused
in the utterance of endless
artifacts with no reason
to be spoken beyond the
disturbing of a doubtful peace.
It is within the catalogue
of permissible things to be
dead wrong and even to derive
moderate pleasure practicing
intransigence for its own sake.

■

When time comes to resume
speaking, say what you have
to say, all at once, letting it be
the lover who speaks, the one who
will most rarely say you wrong;
let the rest be meat for crows.
If no one tried to live this way
no one would discover it can't be done.

These are the things you do
trying to be true whether or
not you know you do. In the
meantime, something's always
creeping up with a good deal
of stealth, usually undetected
until its moment of denouement,
generally after it's perpetrated
some activity so *off the wall* it
could never have been predicted—
such as installing a bidet in the
birdbath . . . or detailing how both
what we did and did not do either
was or was not more or less
than it appeared in light of a
value we had never considered.

Who *we* were meanwhile was
a gaggle of collateral witnesses

providing unnecessary alibis
for a failure we were no longer
perceived as having. Now it was
time to start denying responsibility
for being so disproportionately
large, plead innocence and try to
lay the blame on the times . . .
the old *Aw Shucks* approach,
valid to a degree but more of
a smoke screen than an outright
explanation. The fact is
we no longer fit anywhere
and there's not a great
deal to be said about it that
hasn't been said before though
there's always a chance that
something can be blurted in
a breath that couldn't be
thought out in a thousand years.

Transformation happens when
the old rules don't apply the
way they used to and the new
rules are still being written.

Perception was a creation of the
'60s. There's nothing intelligent
to say about it because intelligence
wasn't invented until the '70s.

Discrimination was the brainchild
of the '80s, the ability to tell a
louse from a Lifesaver. Meanwhile
here in the '90s we seem to be
chewing on the notion of synthesis,
which is probably a good thing
because it provides a new context
that'll fit just about anything that
the tides of the times wash up
on the gut-infested shore and
decline to wash back out again.

Grab a quick nap approaching
extinction out of a great gray
steel-faced shutter to awake with
the time almost entirely gone,
sliced into slivers thinner than
seconds and served between
draughts of black brew from a
cornucopia connected to the
sludge at the floor of the sea
where Monkey Face sinks to
shine between ambiguities.

No chance to enclose anything
in the shaft of an oversize arrow
except for this ridiculous rose
carved from a ruby as large as

a fist, odorless and semi-eternal,
while upon the strongbox the
new Queen of Hearts stares
straight ahead at the horizon,
remembering when it stretched
forever, perfectly straight and
endlessly distant, where ships
fell off the edge of the world.

Attempts to rephrase the
old equations for balance
and proportion dissolve like
slugs in salt for reasons
no one cares to consider.
That would be looking back
and we know better, how it
tends to devour whatever
small personal space remains;
how the Trope of Eternity
surfaces at odd junctures
to bathe in the soup without
so much as phoning ahead,
tells you it was at your own
invitation and *proves* it.

Whoever said life is a bowl
of fruit *of any kind* never
understood the intricacies

of angling for a fish as big
as New Jersey without bait.

Someone else has to care
as much for your unspoken
promise as you do if hope
is to be regulated in any
deeply satisfying way—
things don't tend to work
like that so you learn to
cling to the diminishing
number of artifacts that
testify to the truth that you
stumbled on this without
planning or wanting it,
found it ambiguous and
tried to make the best of it.

The facts, if there are any,
will be reassessed at each
change of context; the score
is never exactly tallied and
consequently never settled.

I say *we* or it is the wind who speaks
with loose lips to a mango moon
spilling fermented fragrance over
the woman with amber eyes

gazing into a sine wave generator
saying: "Go on and hypnotize me.
Prove to me there is such a thing.

"Bend me to your will if you can.
Make me demand that you
lay down your life for me.
Make me believe. Without details,
Above all do not trouble me with details . . ."

Permanence is in such short
supply one understandably
wonders what today looks like
twenty-five years down the line;
if the flies get to the rye before
the frost or whether east of the
sun logically becomes west of
the moon in curvaceous space
without the necessity for doing
much more than hanging in there
long enough for it to come around
in its own good time, sweet and
shimmering as love wearing a long
blue cloud in a sweet and spotless sky.

Mama said there'd be days
like this but never how many,
how long and how emphatic.

Which about covers it except
to stress that should the thing
that wants saying not be said
in a breath, so that it steps forth
and *stays* said, accepting the
possibility of being irrevocably wrong,
it might just as well never be said at all.

JESSICA LEOPARD

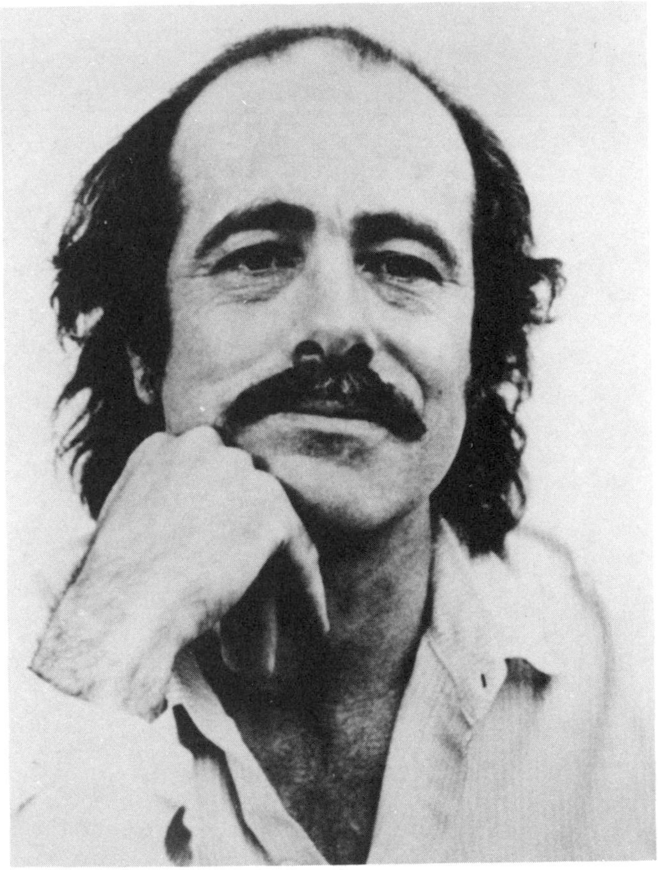

ABOUT THE AUTHOR

Robert Hunter's debut as a poet was the publication of his translation of Rilke's *Duino Elegies* (Hulogosi, 1987). His first collection of poems, *Night Cadre*, was published by Viking Penguin in 1991. The book-length poem *Idiot's Delight* was published by the Hanuman Press in 1992, followed by the collection *Infinity Minus Eleven* (Spike 3) in 1993. His translation of Rilke's *The Sonnets to Orpheus* is scheduled for publication by Hulogosi in the fall of 1993.

For thirty years Hunter has been the primary lyricist for the Grateful Dead. In November 1993 Penguin published *A Box of Rain: Lyrics 1965–1993*.